W9-BDE-262

-ip as in ship

Kelly Doudna

Consulting Editor Monica Marx, M.A./Reading Specialist

Published by SandCastle™, an imprint of ABDO Publishing Company, 4940 Viking Drive, Edina, Minnesota 55435.

Printed in the United States.

Credits
Edited by: Pam Price
Curriculum Coordinator: Nancy Tuminelly
Cover and Interior Design and Production: Mighty Media
Photo Credits: Comstock, Corbis Images, Eyewire Images, Hemera, PhotoDisc, Stockbyte

Library of Congress Cataloging-in-Publication Data

Doudna, Kelly, 1963-
    -Ip as in ship / Kelly Doudna.
        p. cm. -- (Word families. Set III)
    Summary: Introduces, in brief text and illustrations, the use of the letter combination "ip" in such words as "ship," "trip," "whip," and "lip."
    ISBN 1-59197-239-6
    1. Readers (Primary) [1. Vocabulary. 2. Reading.] I. Title.

PE1119 .D67584 2003
428.1--dc21   2002038634

SandCastle™ books are created by a professional team of educators, reading specialists, and content developers around five essential components that include phonemic awareness, phonics, vocabulary, text comprehension, and fluency. All books are written, reviewed, and leveled for guided reading, early intervention reading, and Accelerated Reader® programs and designed for use in shared, guided, and independent reading and writing activities to support a balanced approach to literacy instruction.

Let Us Know

After reading the book, SandCastle would like you to tell us your stories about reading. What is your favorite page? Was there something hard that you needed help with? Share the ups and downs of learning to read. We want to hear from you! To get posted on the ABDO Publishing Company Web site, send us e-mail at:

sandcastle@abdopub.com

SandCastle Level: Beginning

-ip Words

dip

rip

ship

tip

trip

whip

Liz takes a dip in the pool.

Phil hopes Skip won't
rip the towel.

Kip and his family took
a cruise on a ship.

The building looks like
it will tip over.

Britt and her mom are on a fishing trip.

The chef uses a whisk
to whip cream.

10

Chip Takes a Trip

Chip is going on a trip.

Chip wants to sail a ship.

The wind starts to whip.

The ship moves along
at a fast clip.

Chip hopes the sail
won't rip.

The ship begins to tip.

Chip ends up
taking a dip.

Chip gets a grip
on a dolphin named Flip.

Chip decides to skip
the next trip.

The -ip Word Family

Chip	rip
clip	ship
dip	sip
drip	skip
Flip	tip
grip	trip
hip	whip
lip	zip

Glossary

Some of the words in this list may have more than one meaning. The meaning listed here reflects the way the word is used in the book.

chef   the head cook in a kitchen

cream   the liquid fat in whole milk

cruise   to take a vacation on a ship

dip   a short swim

rip   to tear or split apart

whip   to beat something, often eggs or cream, into a foam

whisk   a tool used for whipping eggs or cream

About SandCastle™

A professional team of educators, reading specialists, and content developers created the SandCastle™ series to support young readers as they develop reading skills and strategies and increase their general knowledge. The SandCastle™ series has four levels that correspond to early literacy development in young children. The levels are provided to help teachers and parents select the appropriate books for young readers.

Emerging Readers
(no flags)

Beginning Readers
(1 flag)

Transitional Readers
(2 flags)

Fluent Readers
(3 flags)

These levels are meant only as a guide. All levels are subject to change.

To see a complete list of SandCastle™ books and other nonfiction titles from ABDO Publishing Company, visit www.abdopub.com or contact us at:

4940 Viking Drive, Edina, Minnesota 55435 • 1-800-800-1312 • fax: 1-952-831-1632